101 Life-Changing
Japanese Proverbs

*Wisdom from Ancient Japan, Translated
and Explained*

101 Life-Changing Japanese Proverbs: *Wisdom from Ancient Japan, Translated and Explained*

Cover design by Timothy Brooks

ISBN: [9798288224201]

Disclaimer : *This book is for informational purposes only. While every effort has been made to ensure the accuracy and completeness of the information contained herein, the author and publisher assume no responsibility for errors, inaccuracies, omissions, or any outcomes resulting from the use of this information. The content is provided on an "as-is" basis and does not constitute professional or technical advice. Readers are encouraged to consult official sources and professionals for specific guidance.*

Trademarks : *All brand names and product names used in this book are trademarks, registered trademarks, or trade names of their respective holders. The use of trademarks is for reference only and does not imply any affiliation with or endorsement by the trademark holders.*

For permissions, media inquiries, or publishing opportunities, please contact the author at: sspider1012@gmail.com

千里の道も一歩から
Senri no michi mo ippo kara

Even a journey of a thousand miles

begins with a single step.

To the quiet minds who listen before they speak,
the gentle hands that shape the world with care,
and the patient hearts that find meaning in small things.

And to Japan—
not just the place,
but the spirit
that teaches us that beauty lies in imperfection,
strength grows in silence,
and wisdom walks softly.

Japan is a land where wisdom doesn't shout—it whispers. It lives not in declarations, but in quiet phrases passed from generation to generation. These proverbs, born of rice fields and temples, samurai codes and tea ceremonies, earthquakes and cherry blossoms, reflect a culture deeply attuned to nature, impermanence, humility, and the resilience of the human spirit.

This book is a curated collection of 101 Japanese proverbs that carry not just meaning, but **depth**—the kind of truths that are felt more than heard. Some come from Zen teachings. Others trace back to rural folklore, warrior philosophy, or timeless observations of daily life. Each one has endured because it captures something essential about what it means to live, to struggle, to adapt, and to find peace in the uncontrollable.

Every proverb is presented in English translation, followed by an interpretation designed to draw out its meaning—not as a lecture, but as a reflection. These are not slogans to memorize. They are seeds. Read slowly. Pause often. Let them unfold inside you, as Japanese wisdom often does—not with a spark, but with a quiet flame.

This is not a book of quick fixes or shallow quotes. It is a companion for anyone walking the long road of personal growth, emotional clarity, and soulful living. If the Roman proverbs in our other volume are chiselled from stone, these Japanese ones are written in mist, moonlight, and the hush of snowfall.

May these proverbs bring stillness in chaos, patience in haste, and beauty in simplicity.

1. Nana korobi ya oki
Fall down seven times, get up eight.
Resilience lies at the heart of the Japanese spirit. This proverb reminds us that true strength isn't about never failing, but about rising each time we fall—quietly, firmly, without losing faith in the journey.

---

2. Deru kugi wa utareru
The nail that sticks out gets hammered down.
Conformity is often valued in Japanese culture, and this proverb reflects that tension. It's a warning about standing out too boldly in a society that prizes harmony—but also a subtle prompt to choose your battles wisely.

---

3. I no naka no kawazu taikai wo shirazu
A frog in a well does not know the great ocean.
A mind confined to its own small world cannot grasp the vastness of life. This saying is a gentle call to expand your horizons and not mistake limited experience for universal truth.

---

4. Saru mo ki kara ochiru
Even monkeys fall from trees.
Even the most skilled can fail. No one is above error, and humility is always wise. Failure doesn't erase your worth—it simply reminds you that you're human.

5. Koketsu ni irazunba koji wo ezu

If you do not enter the tiger's cave, you will not catch its cub.

Great rewards require great risks. This is a proverb of courage, urging you to face danger if your goal is worth the fear.

6. Shippai wa seikō no moto

Failure is the foundation of success.

In Japanese thought, failure is not an end but a beginning. Each mistake is a lesson—if you're willing to learn.

7. Mizu ni nagasu

Let it flow with the water.

A lesson in forgiveness and letting go. Like water carrying troubles away, this proverb teaches that some things are best released rather than held onto.

8. Ame futte ji katamaru

After the rain, the ground hardens.

Hardship strengthens character. Just as soil solidifies after a storm, people often emerge tougher and wiser after enduring trials.

9. Raku areba ku ari
Where there is pleasure, there is also pain.
Life is balanced between joy and sorrow. One does not exist without the other. True wisdom lies in accepting both without clinging to either.

---

10. Chiri mo tsumoreba yama to naru
Even dust, when piled up, can become a mountain.
Small efforts, repeated, lead to great achievement. Patience and consistency matter more than grand gestures.

---

11. Isogaba maware
If you rush, go around.
Counterintuitive yet profound: when in haste, slow down. A detour may be the wiser path, avoiding unseen pitfalls.

---

12. En no shita no chikaramochi
A strong person under the floorboards.
An unsung hero—someone who supports others silently without seeking recognition. It's a celebration of humility and service behind the scenes.

---

13. Hana yori dango

Dumplings over flowers.

A humorous but honest take: practicality over beauty. It suggests valuing substance (something you can eat) over style (something merely pleasing to the eye).

---

14. Taisetsu na mono wa me ni mienai

The most important things cannot be seen with the eyes.

Love, kindness, trust—these things have no form, but give life meaning. A deeply spiritual reminder to look beyond the material.

---

15. Ichigo ichie

One time, one meeting.

Every encounter is once-in-a-lifetime. Treasuring the moment honors the impermanence of all things—a core idea in Japanese philosophy.

---

16. Tsuru wa sennen, kame wa mannen

A crane lives a thousand years, a turtle ten thousand.

This expresses longevity, endurance, and blessings of long life. Often used to honor elders or wish someone good fortune.

---

17. Gaman wa kin no hana
Patience is a golden flower.
Patience is not passive—it's graceful strength. This proverb values endurance as a virtue that blossoms beautifully over time.

---

18. Ron yori shōko
Proof over argument.
Don't waste time arguing—show the results. Action and evidence carry more weight than clever words.

---

19. Yudan taiteki
Carelessness is a great enemy.
Complacency invites disaster. This proverb is a sharp reminder to stay alert, especially when things seem easy.

---

20. Tora no i o karite kitsune ga ii
A fox using the tiger's authority.
A warning against those who gain power by borrowing it from others—false leaders and opportunists who roar with another's voice.

---

21. Kawa nagarete taishi o shiru
Watch the river flow, and you will understand great truth.
Nature is a teacher. The flowing river symbolizes time, change, and patience. The more you observe quietly, the more life begins to reveal itself.

---

22. Gō ni ireba gō ni shitagae
When in a village, do as the villagers do.
Adaptation is a survival skill. This proverb emphasizes cultural harmony and the wisdom of aligning with your surroundings—without losing yourself.

---

23. Taigen wa yō wo shirusu
Form reveals function.
Things, and people, are known by what they do. This saying highlights the alignment of inner essence and outer behavior—how truth can be seen through action.

---

24. Zeni no tame ni kao o uru
Selling your face for money.
This is a caution against sacrificing your honor, dignity, or identity for material gain. Some prices are too high, even when paid in gold.

---

25. Hotoke no kao mo san-do made
Even a Buddha's face only endures three slaps.
Patience is a virtue—but not endless. Even the most forgiving person has limits. This serves as a fair warning to not test others beyond their capacity.

---

26. Uma no mimi ni nenbutsu
Buddhist prayers in a horse's ear.
Words of wisdom are useless to those who will not hear them. This proverb speaks to the futility of advising someone who chooses ignorance.

---

27. Kuchi wa wazawai no moto
The mouth is the source of misfortune.
Loose talk, gossip, or arrogance often invite trouble. This is a classic reminder to speak mindfully—because words, once said, cannot be taken back.

---

28. Jinsei wa hyōtan kara koma
Life is like a horse emerging from a gourd.
The unexpected happens. This proverb is about the unpredictable, magical nature of life—how something unlikely can suddenly change everything.

---

29. Inu mo arukeba bō ni ataru

Even a dog, if it walks, will bump into a stick.
When you venture out, things will happen—good or bad. But staying still brings nothing. It's a push toward action, even with risk.

---

30. He no kappa

Like water off a kappa's back.
A kappa (mythical river creature) is never bothered by water—this saying means "it's easy" or "no big deal." A humble way of saying you can handle it.

---

31. Tade kuu mushi mo sukizuki

Even the bugs that eat bitter weeds have their preferences.
Tastes differ. What one person rejects, another may treasure. It's a reminder to honor individuality and not judge another's joy.

---

32. Shiranu ga hotoke

Not knowing is Buddha-like.
Ignorance, in some cases, is peaceful. Sometimes it's better not to know, to avoid unnecessary suffering or judgment. Not all knowledge is a blessing.

---

33. Ichinen no kei wa gantan ni ari
The year's plan starts on New Year's Day.
Intentions set early shape the future. Planning at the beginning leads to steadier progress. A call for discipline and foresight.

---

34. Asu no hyōban yori kyō no hōshi
Service today is better than praise tomorrow.
Action now is worth more than future recognition. It encourages selfless work and focusing on the present contribution over delayed applause.

---

35. Hi wa mata noboru
The sun will rise again.
Even in the darkest moment, light returns. This is a soft promise of renewal—a powerful comfort for those going through grief or setbacks.

---

36. Jinsei wa isshun no yume no gotoshi
Life is but a fleeting dream.
A deeply Zen reflection on impermanence. Life is short, fragile, and dreamlike—so live with intention, knowing it will pass.

---

37. Neko ni koban
Gold coins to a cat.
Giving something precious to someone who doesn't understand its value is pointless. Know your audience, and don't waste pearls on closed minds.

---

38. Kōka hiyō o yomu
Read the cries of the incense.
Subtlety is everything. This proverb alludes to reading unspoken signs, tuning into silence, and being sensitive to the invisible layers of communication.

---

39. Kaze ga fukeba okeya ga mōkaru
When the wind blows, the bucket maker profits.
This is about chain reactions and unexpected consequences. Even small events can trigger distant, unpredictable outcomes—a butterfly effect, Japanese-style.

---

40. Yuuga wa shizukesa no naka ni aru
Elegance exists within quietness.
True grace is not loud. This proverb champions restraint, calmness, and a kind of inner beauty that needs no display.

---

41. Tsuki yoru mo arashi no yoru mo
On moonlit nights and stormy ones alike.
Life offers beauty and chaos alike—don't only live for the good days. This saying reminds us to find meaning in all of life's seasons, not just the peaceful ones.

---

42. Kaji wa isogu bekarazu
Never hurry when fighting a fire.
In crisis, stay calm. Rushing leads to ruin. Even in emergencies, clear thought beats blind speed—a subtle lesson in poised action.

---

43. Tōi mizu wa kawa no ryū o sukuwazu
Distant water cannot quench a nearby fire.
Help delayed or too far away is of no use. This emphasizes the importance of timely, present support over distant promises.

---

44. Wasureta koro ni yatte kuru
It comes when you've forgotten about it.
Things—good and bad—tend to arrive when least expected. A warning and a hope all at once, this teaches acceptance of life's surprises.

---

45. Ugokanu yama mo toki ni wa ugoku
Even the unmoving mountain shifts in time.
Change is inevitable, even for what seems eternal. Be patient—stubborn circumstances, people, or obstacles do eventually shift.

---

46. Yokei na osewa wa jama
Unasked help becomes a hindrance.
Kindness without consent can become interference. This is a cultural lesson in restraint, boundaries, and quiet respect.

---

47. Fukō wa renzoku suru
Misfortune comes in chains.
When one trouble comes, others follow. But this proverb also implies the value of vigilance—recognizing patterns can help you prepare and endure.

---

48. Inu no me ni mo namida
Even a dog has tears.
Compassion is not exclusive to humans. This reminds us that all creatures feel pain, and empathy should extend beyond just people.

---

49. Zen wa isoge

Rush to do good.

When it comes to kindness or moral acts, don't delay. Life is uncertain—do what is right while you have the chance.

---

50. Dango yori odango

Prefer dumplings over theatrics.

Sometimes translated as "actions over decoration," this version champions practical results over superficial charm.

---

51. Hito no furi mite waga furi naose

Watch others' behavior and correct your own.

A proverb about learning through observation. Seeing others' mistakes or virtues should be a mirror, not a judgment.

---

52. Ku wa raku no tan

Hardship is the seed of ease.

Suffering often precedes relief. It's not a punishment, but a prelude. This captures the cyclical nature of struggle and peace.

---

53. Tomo wa shinrai kara hajimaru
Friendship begins with trust.
Relationships are rooted not in likeness or fun, but trust.
Without it, friendship is merely proximity, not connection.

---

54. Seisei dōdō to ikiru
Live with dignity and honor.
This is not about pride, but about living transparently,
without deceit or shame. A guiding principle for character.

---

55. Hitokoto wa shiju no doku
A single word can poison a lifetime.
Words matter. A careless insult or harsh remark can leave
scars far beyond the moment. Speak with care.

---

56. Kusa no ne mo negai o motsu
Even the roots of grass have wishes.
Even the smallest, most overlooked beings carry dreams
and hopes. This encourages empathy for all forms of life.

---

57. Kanashimi wa kaze no gotoku
Sorrow passes like the wind.
Pain, no matter how fierce, will move on. This is a gentle whisper of hope for those caught in grief.

---

58. Ichinichi ichinichi ga isshō
Each day is a whole life.
Live each day with intention, as if it were complete in itself. A deeply Zen-inspired call to presence and mindfulness.

---

59. Hō wa tsuyoku, hane wa karui
The law is strong, but feathers are light.
Power doesn't always come with weight. Even what is light or soft can overcome what is rigid. A nod to quiet strength.

---

60. Kokoro wa fukaku, kotoba wa karuku
Let your heart be deep and your words be light.
Be thoughtful inside, gentle outside. This elegant balance between internal gravity and external grace defines much of Japanese aesthetics and interaction.

---

61. Inochi atte no monodane
Everything begins with life itself.
Before wealth, status, or dreams—life must first exist. This proverb is a quiet gratitude for being alive and a reminder not to take that for granted.

62. Kōun wa nezumi no ana kara
Good fortune comes from a mouse hole.
Blessings may emerge from unexpected, even humble places. Never overlook small chances—they may lead to great changes.

63. Hi no nai tokoro ni kemuri wa tatanai
Where there is no fire, there is no smoke.
Rumors often have a seed of truth. This proverb encourages discernment—don't believe everything, but don't ignore signs either.

64. Tsutawareba, yamai mo naoru
If spoken, even illness can be cured.
Sharing pain lightens its burden. Whether it's emotional or physical, expressing what's inside is often the beginning of healing.

65. Toki wa kane nari

Time is money.
Though the phrase feels global now, in Japanese context it underscores discipline, not greed. Time misused is potential lost.

---

66. Tsuki to suppon

The moon and a softshell turtle.
Used to describe two things that are completely different—like night and day, beauty and awkwardness. It's a poetic way of saying: these don't compare.

---

67. Toranu tanuki no kawa zan'yō

Don't count a raccoon's pelt before catching it.
Don't plan your profits before securing the deal. It's the Japanese version of "don't count your chickens before they hatch."

---

68. Te ni ireba raku, ushinau wa yaya yasushi

Gaining is hard, losing is easy.
This sharp truth reminds us that building anything worthwhile—trust, success, love—takes effort. Losing it may take just one moment.

---

69. Jinsei wa hana no yō ni hakanai
Life is as fleeting as a flower.
A classic reflection on impermanence. Even the most beautiful moments, like blossoms, must fall. It's the transience that gives life meaning.

---

70. Tatsu tori ato o nigosazu
A departing bird does not muddy the water.
Leave cleanly. Whether exiting a job, relationship, or phase of life, do so with grace and no lingering mess. Part of honor is in how you end things.

---

71. Kage no nai hito wa inai
There is no person without a shadow.
Everyone has flaws, regrets, or hidden struggles. This is a reminder to judge less and empathize more—perfection is an illusion.

---

72. Kaze o hiku toki wa taorete yokei ni tsuyoi
A tree falls harder when it's been weakened by wind.
We ignore our strain until we collapse. Take care of your stress before it breaks you—prevention is strength.

---

73. Oishii mono ni wa doku ga aru
Delicious things often carry poison.
Pleasure isn't always good for you. Whether food, fame, or flattery—this is a warning against indulgence without discernment.

---

74. Soko ga mieru to wa, mada fukai
If you think you see the bottom, it's still deep.
Understanding is deeper than it appears. Don't mistake glimpses for total truth—wisdom is humble before mystery.

---

75. Ningen banji saiō ga uma
In all human affairs, the old man and his horse.
Based on a famous story: a misfortune becomes a blessing, then a blessing becomes misfortune. You never really know what's good or bad—so stay steady.

---

76. Uso mo hōben
Even lies can be a means to an end.
This isn't permission for deceit, but an acknowledgement that in some situations, gentler truths—or strategic silence—serve compassion.

---

77. Zuihitsu no gotoku ikiru
Live like an essay with no outline.
A reference to the Japanese literary form *zuihitsu*, which flows naturally from one thought to another. This proverb celebrates living freely, responsively, not rigidly.

---

78. Kaji mo jinsei mo fuki nagara yokei mo eru
Both fire and life spread more when fanned.
Energy follows attention. What you feed with effort or emotion will grow—whether passion or pain. Choose your focus wisely.

---

79. Ko o mite oya o shiru
You understand the parent by observing the child.
Children reflect what they're taught. This is both a compliment and a caution to parents—your values echo through generations.

---

80. Kokoro ni ame, soto wa hare
Rain inside the heart, clear skies outside.
A poignant image of silent sorrow. Someone may seem fine on the outside, yet be grieving within. Never assume others aren't suffering just because they smile.

---

81. Yoru no tsuru wa naku oto sae utsukushii

Even the night crane's cry is beautiful.

Even sorrow or loneliness, when embraced, can have its own kind of grace. This speaks to the subtle beauty found in melancholy and solitude.

82. Haji wa kakinemo naranai

Shame cannot be wiped away like ink.

Once your honor is stained, it's difficult to erase. A cautionary reminder of the weight our choices carry.

83. Hana wa sakihokoru toki yori chiru toki utsukushii

A flower is more beautiful when it falls than when it blooms.

There is unmatched elegance in graceful decline or endings. This reflects Japanese aesthetics of *wabi-sabi*: beauty in transience.

84. Neko wa shiranai furi o suru

A cat pretends not to know.

Sometimes people feign ignorance as a form of subtle resistance or wisdom. Not all silence is stupidity— sometimes it's strategy.

85. Hibi kore kōjitsu
Every day is a good day.
A Zen expression that invites presence. Even when nothing goes "right," the mere act of living fully is enough to bless the day.

---

86. Ten yori shidai
Leave it to heaven.
When things are beyond your control, surrender. Trusting the flow of fate is not weakness—it's peaceful wisdom.

---

87. Yubi sasu hō ga itai
The finger that points feels the pain.
Judging others wounds the one who judges. This is a quiet spiritual insight: projection often reveals our own shadows.

---

88. I no naka no kawazu taikai o shirazu
The frog in the well does not know the ocean.
A well-known Japanese metaphor for limited perspective. Don't confuse your bubble for the world. Seek experience beyond comfort.

---

89. Tōi michi wa chikamichi kara
A long journey begins with a shortcut.
The path to mastery often begins in impatience—but true wisdom is learning to go slowly. Rushing reveals what you still lack.

---

90. Karui kotoba wa omoi kokoro o arawasu
Light words can reveal a heavy heart.
Sometimes what seems casual hides deep pain. Listen carefully—not just to what is said, but to what isn't.

---

91. En wa isogaba maware
If in a hurry, take the longer route.
Patience often gets you there faster. A crooked, considered road beats a reckless straight one. This is life's quiet efficiency.

---

92. Hitotsu no tsubomi mo haru o shiraseru
Even one bud announces spring.
Small signs point to great changes. A single improvement, word, or gesture may carry the promise of a whole new season.

---

93. Saki ni tateru wa tame ni nari

To bow first is to lead.
Initiating kindness, humility, or respect is not weakness—
it's leadership. This reveals the power in going first when
no one else does.

---

94. Ame furu kara kaze ga tatsu

Rain brings wind.
Trouble often follows trouble—but also, some
disturbances are needed to stir change. Storms may
awaken something still inside you.

---

95. Yasashisa wa tsuyosa no shirushi

Kindness is a sign of strength.
True power is gentle. Those who are secure have no need
to dominate. This is a quiet rebellion against cruelty
disguised as toughness.

---

96. Ue o mireba kiri ga nai

Looking up, there is no end.
Ambition is infinite—but it can also leave you dissatisfied.
Be grateful, even as you grow. Comparison steals peace.

---

97. Kurayami ni sashikomu hikari wa tsuyoi

The light that enters darkness is strongest.
Hope that survives despair is the most powerful kind. A reminder that breakthrough comes from within the shadow, not beyond it.

98. Te no hira no ue no unmei

Destiny rests in the palm of your hand.
You have more agency than you think. Though fate exists, it dances with your decisions. You are not powerless.

99. Dōro wa jibun de tsukuru mono

The road is something you create yourself.
Don't wait for a path—make one. This encourages boldness, creativity, and the courage to walk where none have yet.

100. Kokoro o tojitara sekai mo tozaru

When the heart is closed, so is the world.
An inwardly shut person sees no joy, no beauty. The world changes not by force—but by how we choose to open ourselves to it.

101. Iki wa hitotsu no okurimono

Breath is a single gift.

Life, at its core, is just this breath—this moment. The simplest thing we ignore is the greatest treasure. Remember to breathe.

About the Author

Maxwell W. Wilson is a passionate lifelong learner with a background in Information Technology and Contemporary Marketing. He believes that knowledge should be both enlightening and enjoyable—a philosophy he brings into every book he writes. For Maxwell, writing is more than just sharing information; it's about creating a journey where readers engage, learn, and have fun. His commitment to rigorous research ensures that every detail is spot-on, while his lively writing style keeps readers captivated. Whether you're diving into new concepts or brushing up on the familiar, Maxwell's books promise an experience that's both informative and refreshingly entertaining.

For a behind-the-scenes look at Maxwell's latest thoughts and projects, you can find him on Instagram under the handle **@anotsowiseoldman**.

Made in United States
Orlando, FL
02 July 2025

62551487R00022